Once there was a girl who needed to write a letter to someone very special but she could not find the words.

So she went to her favorite bench at her favorite park and waited for the words to find her instead...

"Dear You," she wrote and waited... but the words would not come.
"I know!" she thought after some time, "I'll go for a walk, maybe the
I will find the words.

So she got up and walked away not realizing that she had forgotten her letter on the bench!

Just then, the wind blew with a WHOOSH,
picking up the letter and blowing it into a tree!

Later, an old woman walked by and saw the letter in the tree and was curious what it said...

...She almost couldn't reach the letter, but after trying her very best, she pulled it down!

The old woman pulled a pencil out of her purse, thought for a while, and wrote some words.

Then she put down the paper, stood up slowly, and walked away.

Some time passed and the wind continued to blow lightly in the park, moving the letter from here to there and back again, finally settling down on the ground beside the bench.

Just then, a young girl riding her bike in the park rode by and noticed the paper on the ground, so she stopped with a SCREECH and picked it up.

As she read the letter, she wondered who it could be written to. "Whoever it is must be very special" she thought.

Then, with a smile, she dashed to her bike, pulled out a crayon, and sat on the bench.

Slowly and carefully, she wrote each word as perfectly as she could. When she was done, she put the letter back on the bench, climbed on her bike, and rode away.

The leaves were falling from the trees and, as the girl rode away,
a man with a leaf blower came by to clean the park.

As he cleaned the park the man did not see the letter and accidentally blew it high into another tree where it could not be reached!

Seeing this, a little bird that was sitting on the lamp post flew over
as fast as she could, picked up the paper...

...And returned it to the bench below.

As the letter slowly fell towards the bench, a man jogging in the park ran by.

Before he could realize it, the letter had hit the man in the face!
"What is this?!" he thought.

As he read the letter, words came to him that he wished he had told someone very special but never did.

So, pulling a marker out of his pocket, he wrote down those words, put the letter down on the bench and jogged away.

Once again, the leaves began to rustle and move...
the wind was going to blow again!

And with a mighty WHOOSH, the wind picked up
the letter and let it go above a pond near the bench!

When a frog in the pond saw that the letter was going to land in the water, he jumped in the air and caught the letter in his mouth making sure to keep it dry.

Then, carefully and quickly, he hopped to the bench, set the letter down, and hopped back to join his friends in the pond.

The sun was now coming down and the day was almost done, as a woman walked by the bench pushing her baby for an evening walk.

Seeing the letter, she reached down, picked it up, and began to read.

Knowing exactly what she wanted to say, she smiled at her baby,
wrote some words and set the letter back down on the bench.

The park was very quiet now as the sun had gone down and the animals had all gone to sleep.

Just then, the girl who could not find the words walked by once again and saw her letter sitting on the bench.

As she sat down, reading the words on the paper, she could not believe her eyes. The words were there, exactly how she had wanted to say them. They had found her after all and the letter was perfect!

So, with a smile on her face and a tear in her eye, she simply signed 'Love always, Me,' and sent the letter away.

Dear You,

You are perfect. Never let anyone tell you otherwise. Be who you are, and be proud of who that is. God made you exactly how you are supposed to be, quirks and all.

Help people you don't know and never hesitate to offer kindness, even when people don't offer it back to you. Life is about what you give, not what you get so be generous.

Be silly. Laugh every day. ask questions and don't worry about things that you kant change forgive quickly and lern from your mistakes!

You are loved by more people than you will ever know, and thought about often by people you wouldn't expect. I know this because I am one of those people.

Live life and be thankfull for the little things. Every day is a blessing never forget that.

Love always,
Me